HANDY POCKET GUIDE

QUILTER'S
FABRIC

A

Tips
Selection, Care & Storage

C&T PUBLISHING

contents

FABRIC AND COLOR:

CHOOSE IT AND USE IT!

A huge common element that binds quilters together is our passion for fabric.

No surprise here: *Fabric is our lifeline to creativity.*

FABRIC GRAIN

Selvages   When fabric is produced, the threads are woven in two directions, creating a lengthwise and crosswise grain. The long, finished edges of the fabric are called the selvages.

Straight of grain   The lengthwise and crosswise grain is called the straight of grain. The lengthwise grain runs parallel to the selvages and has little, if any stretch. The crosswise grain, which runs across the fabric from selvage to selvage, has a little stretch.

Bias   The bias, which runs diagonally across the fabric in any direction, has lots of stretch. Because of this, handle any bias edges—whether cutting them, sewing them, or pressing them—very carefully to avoid distortion.

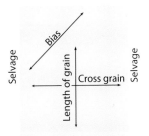

LET'S SHOP!

New fabrics continue to appear in the marketplace, and we quilters *do* love the new stuff! Colors and styles come and go, and it's always a good idea to take advantage of the opportunities when we see them. An infusion of even a few trendy colors and prints can add freshness to your quilt.

I'm always on the lookout for fabrics to expand and enrich my stash, and when I find something I like or that I know will fill a gap in my collection, I buy at least ⅓ yard. If I find a print that has the potential to become the foundation for a quilt—for example, a promising focus fabric—I guesstimate enough for a border and then add an additional ½ yard, just in case. (If nothing else, I know I can use the yardage for backing.)

When determining your own shopping guidelines, budget and storage space will, of course, come into play, as will the size quilts you usually make. A quilter who leans toward king- or queen-size projects will probably buy more fabric—either in variety or quantity—than one who rarely makes anything larger than a wall quilt.

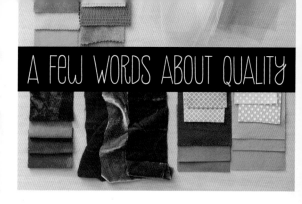

A FEW WORDS ABOUT QUALITY

For the most part, I recommend that you work with the best 100% cotton fabric available from your local quilt shop. Fabric of lesser quality—for example, with a looser weave, with a lower thread count, or the result of improper processing—might ravel, stretch, or distort, making accurate piecing and smooth appliqué difficult, if not impossible. A great deal of work goes into making a quilt, and your time is worth the best materials available. I would rather have five pieces of quality fabric than twenty pieces of lesser quality.

TIP

You may also want to play with many "nontraditional fabrics." Today's quilters love voile and wool and silk ... and more! I recommend that you work with quality fabrics in these alternatives as well. (See Nontraditional Fabrics, page 36, for specifics about these fabrics.)

THREE KEYS to SUCCESSFUL FABRIC SELECTION

Whether you're gathering fabrics for your very first quilt or you're a long-time quilter working on building a healthy fabric collection, the same basic principles apply. Aim for a good mix of color, value, and character of print.

COLOR

When we speak of a color, we're speaking of that color's *entire family*—and color families can be quite large. They include all the lights and darks, tints and shades of that particular family.

Meet the Red family!

Don't be afraid to open yourself to *all* the colors available to you, not just the ones that you love and that you've always been drawn to. As you continue to grow your fabric stash, keep an eye out for the colors that are missing from your collection and make a note to hunt them down next time you head to your favorite fabric source. Your future quilts will love you for it!

If you look at old quilts, you'll often find colors, or combinations of colors, that would never cross your mind as candidates for your next quilting project. Our foremothers (and, occasionally, forefathers) were fearless; they worked with rich red, electric blue, bile green, bubblegum pink, citrus yellow, cheddar orange—sometimes all in the same quilt—and we're still admiring these quilts more than 125 years later.

Fabrics in colors reminiscent of vintage quilts from the Late 1800s

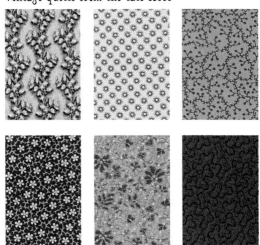

WORKING THE WHEEL

When I'm stumped for a color scheme, feel my palette would benefit from the addition of another color (or colors), or wonder if the colors I'm considering will play well together, I look to the color wheel. It's a great guide for determining successful color relationships, especially when you're expanding your horizons to work with colors you might not have worked with before.

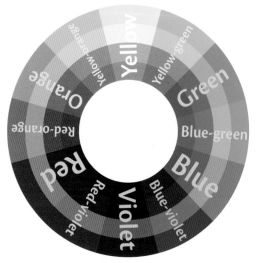

COLOR WHEEL

Here are a few basic **color schemes** that you can draw from the color wheel.

Monochromatic   This color scheme showcases a single color family in all its glory—for example, a blue color scheme can include blues from the palest baby blue to deep, rich navy.

Complementary   This color scheme is built around two color families that appear opposite each other on the color wheel, such as red and green.

Triadic   This color scheme is built around three color families that are equally distant from each other on the wheel, such as yellow-orange, red-violet, and blue-green. To find a triadic color scheme, start with a single color on the wheel, and—moving clockwise—skip three colors, select the next, skip three more, and select the next color. Skip another three colors and you're back to your starting point, creating a perfect triadic color scheme.

Analogous   This color scheme is made up of neighbors on the color wheel and can include three, four, or more side-by-side color families. This is one of the easiest and most relaxing schemes to work with, as each color contains some element of its immediate neighbors, and the colors flow seamlessly, one to the next.

VALUE

Value refers to the relative lightness or darkness of a fabric. You'll want to be certain that you have a good range of values—light to dark—of every color in both your quilt and your stash. A range of values is what transforms a color into a color family.

The key word in the definition of value is *relative*. You can't tell how light or dark a fabric is when you look at it by itself. It all depends upon the other fabrics that surround it in the block or quilt.

For example, in a Star block, the star points define the star image. If you place the fabric with the strongest contrast in value—say, the darkest fabric—in the "point position," there'll be no missing your intent. On the other hand, place that dark fabric in the center of the star, and that's where your eye will go. Set a bunch of these blocks together, and your Star quilt will read as a sea of big, dark squares.

Even though some of the star-point fabrics in these blocks are not super dark, they are always *relatively* darker than the fabrics I used for the star centers and background, so the stars come shining through.

CHARACTER OF PRINT

Character of print refers to the figures or motifs that appear on a printed fabric. (Some quilters call this "visual texture"—same thing.) As with color and value, you'll want your quilt and your fabric collection to include a good mix of prints. Here are some examples.

Florals

Plaids

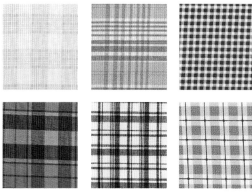

Dots

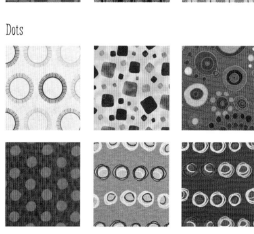

Feathers and paisleys

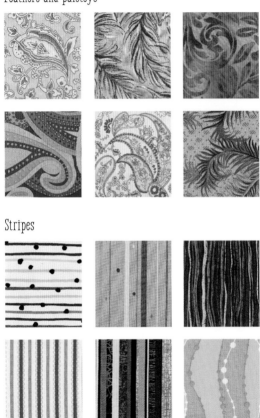

Stripes

Swirls and twirls

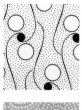

Picture prints

Geometrics

Organics/foliage

Nature's bounty

TIP

Don't be afraid of large-scale and otherwise unusual fabric designs. You'll be cutting these fabrics into small pieces, and the results can be surprising. A window template, tailored to the size and shape of the piece you'll be cutting, will give you a good preview.

A window template gives you a unique perspective on large-scale or otherwise unusual prints.

ADD SOME SPARKLE

Before we move on, I want to put in a word for what I call sparkle and bridge fabrics.

Sparkle fabrics are typically monochromatic prints that include the complete range of value—light to dark—of their particular color family; sometimes they include bits of white as well. You'll love the crispness these lively prints add to your quilt.

Sparkle fabrics add personality and visual texture to your quilt.

Bridge fabrics are also usually monochromatic prints that have several color variations from within a single color family. These fabrics ease the transition when you're using many variations of one color family within your quilt. Notice how the fabric used for the top bar shown below pulls all the different colors within the family together.

The fabric in the top bar is the bridge fabric.

ALTERNATIVE STRATEGIES FOR CHOOSING FABRICS

FABULOUS FOCUS FABRIC (OR FAVORITE DESIGNER)

A focus fabric is a multicolored, often large-scale print that you can build a color scheme—and a quilt—around. In short, the fabric designer has done the heavy lifting for you. Study the colors in the focus fabric, pull a variety of fabrics in those colors from your stash, check that they include a good range of values and character of print, and you're ready to go.

Occasionally, a designer comes along whose fabrics just speak to me, and I find myself adding more and more of that designer's pieces to my stash. Over time, that area of my collection grows to include "vintage" pieces from that designer's various fabric lines, as well as his or her newest creations. My guess is that you have your favorite designers (or fabric lines) too … and they make another great starting point for a super quilt.

Baskets (56″ × 56″), designed and made by Alex Anderson, machine quilted by Diana Johnson

My focus fabric for this quilt was the large-scale multi-colored print that I used for the border.

TIP

If you're building your quilt around a focus fabric, purchase enough for a potential border. If you don't use it there, you can use it for backing.

CAPTURE A STYLE OR AN ERA

Given my love for vintage quilts, it's not surprising that some of my favorite quilts are those that replicate the look or style of a particular time period. With so many luscious reproduction fabrics available, it's fun—and easy—to make a quilt that looks as though it were fashioned in the nineteenth century or created during the height of the 1930s quilt revival.

Wheels and Fans (76″ × 76″), designed and made by Alex Anderson, hand quilted by Amish quilters.

This quilt was built around my treasured stash of feedsacks and 1930s reproduction fabrics.

CARING FOR FABRIC

You've got your fabric home. Now what do you do with it? Given its importance, it's no wonder that we have so many questions when it comes to the proper care of our beloved fabrics.

TO PREWASH ... OR NOT?

Perhaps first and foremost when working with quilting cotton is the question: to prewash or not? I can guarantee that you'll get a *very* different answer depending upon whom you ask; be assured, there is not a gentle divide between "yes" and "no." The sentiment is usually—shall I put this delicately?—very strong one way or the other, and either way, the individual responding can offer you some very clear-cut reasons for the response. That said, here are my thoughts regarding this sensitive hot spot in the land of quilting wisdom.

In general, my philosophy is to prewash, and here's why:

- At its first washing, 100% cotton fabric has a tendency to shrink a bit. Better it shrinks before than after it goes into your quilt.

- Dyes from darker fabrics have been known to migrate (or bleed) into lighter fabrics. Ouch!

- Fabric can gather dust while sitting on the quilt shop's shelves or while waiting in your stash. It is also treated with various chemicals during the production process—chemicals I'd prefer not to inhale or touch.

TIP

Some quilters prefer the crisp feel of unwashed fabric and argue that this crispness is lost when the fabric is laundered before being cut and sewn. Here's a solution. If the fabric seems excessively "limp" after washing, use a *light touch* of spray starch or sizing on the fabric when pressing it afterward. Keep in mind that when you make this choice, you're also making the commitment to wash the finished quilt to remove any product residue.

Still on the fence? Consider how the finished quilt will be used. Chances are, if you're making the quilt for use on a bed or by a child, at some time that quilt will need to be laundered. Best to wash the fabrics now so there are no problems later. This is even more critical if you are giving the quilt as a gift and have no control over its future "life." Prewash now and tuck instructions for aftercare into the box with your quilted gift. If your quilt is purely decorative and will likely never require immersion, you may decide to skip the suds.

TIPS FOR (FABRIC) LAUNDRY DAY

Here are some tips for prewashing your fabrics before using them in your quilt.

• Completely unfold the fabric before placing it in the sink, tub, or washing machine.

• Always wash light and dark fabrics separately.

• Wash your fabrics using the same water temperature and with the same gentle detergent you would use for your best cotton clothing.

• Leave the selvages intact until you've washed the fabric and make a small snip in each corner of the piece before popping it into the washing machine. This helps keep the edges of the fabric from raveling as the fabric is agitated.

- Use a small bag, suitable for laundering delicate lingerie, for washing especially small pieces of fabric.

- Remove fabrics from the dryer as soon as the drying process is complete. (Some quilters even remove the fabrics while still slightly damp.) This makes pressing so much easier!

- Although hand-dyed fabric goes through many immersions in the dyeing process, always test-wash your purchased hand dyes at home before you use them. Water is treated differently in different places, and fabric that ran clear for the dyer may still give off color in *your* water. Better to be safe than sorry!

TROUBLESHOOTING:
TRIAGE FOR BLEEDING FABRIC

If you choose not to prewash, you should at least test your fabric for colorfastness.

Place a 2″ square of test fabric in boiling water. If the color runs off into the water, repeat the process. If it no longer bleeds, you can use it in your quilt, but you will need to prewash the remainder to feel confident in using it. If it continues to discharge color after multiple soakings, save it for a project that will not be laundered.

The experience of having the colors in unwashed fabric run (or bleed) when the finished quilt is laundered—or even dampened or sprayed to remove any marking—defines the word heartbreak. Even if you've never experienced it, I'm sure you've heard the sad, sad stories. I am particularly cautious of reds and red-based colors, such as purple, that have a lot of red in them, but I have also learned to be cautious of even more "innocent" colors.

Some wonderful products on the market can help resolve the problems of bleeding fabric, either in the prewash stage or in a finished quilt.

Synthrapol releases and suspends excess dye molecules in the water so that they pass safely down the drain. This product is particularly great for laundering hand-dyed fabrics. It also can be effective when laundering a finished quilt, keeping loose dye particles in suspension so they don't creep into other areas of the quilt.

Retayne is used to set dye, primarily in commercial fabrics. It increases the size of the dye molecules so they get "wedged" into the fiber. You might want to consider prewashing your quilting fabrics with Synthrapol and then using Retayne to set the color in the final wash.

Many quilters swear by **Shout Color Catchers**, which are readily available at supermarkets where you typically find laundry products. When used during the washing process, these "magic sheets" act like a sponge to attract and soak up excess dye in the wash water.

My advice? Experiment with the options available to see which products you like best and which work best for you in a given situation.

WHERE AND HOW TO STORE FABRIC

There are a million ways to store fabric; however, first and foremost, it should be kept away from a light source—natural or artificial—to avoid fading. Second, your fabric should be easy to access. If it's an effort to pull out your fabric to play with, most likely you won't bother.

I removed the doors from my sewing-room closet, purchased a spring rod, installed pull-out wire baskets, and made a split curtain to protect the fabric from the light.

I sort my fabrics by color families, with odd fabrics that don't fit a family, such as multicolored focus fabrics, novelty prints, or plaids, each stored in a separate bin. I fold the fabrics and store them on end, which makes them easy to sort through to find just the right one. I use an old suitcase as a catchall for my smallest scraps.

Another option is to purchase lidded boxes from a business or home storage company, label the boxes, and use these for storage. Avoid plastic bags; you want your precious fabrics to breathe.

You can sort and store fabrics by color, by style, by era (nineteenth-century reproductions, 1930s prints), by use (focus or border fabrics), or even by designer.

NONTRADITIONAL FABRICS

Using noncotton fabrics in patchwork quilting has a long history. In the late 1700s (and beyond) patchwork quilts often mixed wool, silk, linen, and cotton in the same piece. Utilitarian and functional quilts often used whatever was on hand from clothing to linens to burlap and other packaging materials (think "feedsacks," which started out as canvas bags and later became cotton). Crazy quilters have always used silks and satins and velvets along with home decor or other decorative fabrics.

Care and use   In general, if you are going to use a mixture of different fabrics or different weights of fabrics in the same quilt, it's important to prewash them all the way the finished quilt will get washed. If you are using a fabric that ravels, such as linen, consider overstitching the edges after cutting. In your planning, keep in mind that thicker fabrics, such as denim and broadcloth, are more bulky in seams and harder to stitch through (avoid hand stitching and quilting). When working with any fabric that is "fragile" (such as silk), a lightweight stabilizer ironed onto the back will help solve multiple issues.

The organic thing   There are a number of manufacturers now using 100% certified organic cotton in their base cloths. The fabrics are considered better for the environment. Organic cotton can be found in many different fabrics, including quilting weight, broadcloth, denim, double gauze, and more.

Flannel

Wool

Denim

Lawn

Knits

Voile

Today, mainstream quilting-weight cotton alternatives abound. Here are some options:

Flannel   Made from brushed cotton, flannel is soft and makes a great backing to quilts. Flannel shrinks and can stretch.

Wool   This natural fiber that comes from sheep and other animals is warm and durable. Felted wools won't ravel and are great choices for raw-edge appliqué when sewn onto wool (such as in traditional penny rugs) or paired with cotton. Unfelted wool will shrink.

Denim   A staple in "repurposed-material" quilts, this cotton fabric can come from old jeans or off the bolt. Don't try to hand piece or quilt these quilts!

Lawn   This semi-sheer fabric is often made from cotton, which does shrink. It has a smooth finish and nice drape, like voile.

Knits   The stretchy and soft quality of knits that make the fabric ideal for clothing make it less than perfect for quilting. That's not to say you shouldn't use it! You just need to use an iron-on interfacing (such as Stabili-TEE Fusible Interfacing by C&T Publishing) on the back.

Voile   This thin cotton fabric is lightweight and has soft hand and a nice drape. Many fabric designers are including voile collections to mix and match with their quilting cottons. It can slip during sewing, so use a lot of pins.

Double gauze

Broadcloth

Silk

Linen

Double gauze   The two layers of gauze fabric tacked together give this fabric its name. It's very soft and perfect for swaddling blankets and other items made for baby.

Broadcloth   Often in cotton or a variety of cotton blends, broadcloths are stiffer than traditional quilting cottons.

Silk   There are many different types of silks to play with. They have different sheens and hands. Dupioni silk doesn't shift (or feel as "slippery") as other silks, acting more like cotton. Use a sharp needle when sewing and a low-temperature iron when pressing. Consider using a lightweight fusible fabric prep before cutting the desired shapes, because many silks ravel at the edges.

Linen   Often paired with cotton in patchwork quilts, this fabric made from flax plant fibers is woven in different weights. It shrinks, wrinkles, and ravels but can be worth the care and effort for its beautiful, natural appearance and texture. There are also lines of cotton/linen blends to explore.

Home decor There are a variety of home decor fabrics, and the most relatable for quilting is decor-weight cotton. It's stiffer than quilting-weight cotton and great for bags and accessories. It can be used in quilts but the seams will be bulkier and is probably not the best for piecing intricate blocks.

Velvet This soft fabric is often used in crazy quilts and has a distinctive nap. The material is called *velvet* when made from silk and *velveteen* when made from cotton. Be careful when pressing velvets, that the iron does not hurt the fuzzy surface.

Minky Super soft and furry, this nonwoven fabric can be tricky to sew because of the nap. Pinning closely and using a walking foot will allow you to try this luxuriously cozy fabric on the back of a lap quilt.

Crazy Quilt Sewing Pouch
from *Foolproof Crazy-Quilt Projects*
by Jennifer Clouston (available from C&T Publishing)

Text copyright © 2017 by Alex Anderson
Photography and artwork copyright © 2017 by C&T Publishing, Inc.

Publisher: Amy Marson

Creative Director: Gailen Runge

Project Editor: Alice Mace Nakanishi

Developmental Editor: Liz Aneloski

Technical Editor: Nan Powell

Cover/Book Designer: Kerry Graham

Production Coordinator: Zinnia Heinzmann

Photographers: Diane Pedersen, Nissa Brehmer, Christina
Carty-Francis, Luke Mulks, Sharon Risedorph, John Bagley,
and Richard Tauber, unless otherwise noted

Published by C&T Publishing, Inc., P.O. Box 1456, Lafayette, CA 94549

We take great care to ensure that the information included in our
products is accurate and presented in good faith, but no warranty
is provided, nor are results guaranteed. Neither the author nor
C&T Publishing, Inc., shall have any liability to any person or entity
with respect to any loss or damage caused directly or indirectly
by the information contained in this book. For your convenience,
we post an up-to-date listing of corrections on our website
(ctpub.com). If a correction is not already noted, please contact our
customer service department at ctinfo@ctpub.com or P.O. Box 1456,
Lafayette, CA 94549.

Trademark (™) and registered trademark (®) names are used
throughout this book. Rather than use the symbols with every
occurrence, we are using the names only in the editorial fashion and
to the benefit of the owner, with no intention of infringement.

Printed in China

10 9 8 7 6 5 4 3 2 1

ABOUT THE AUTHOR

Alex Anderson seeks to educate, entertain, and grow today's quilting community. Longtime host of the television show *Simply Quilts*, she is also an executive producer and cohost of *The Quilt Show* with Ricky Tims. Visit Alex on the web at alexandersonquilts.com.

Notes

Notes

- -